KU-159-522

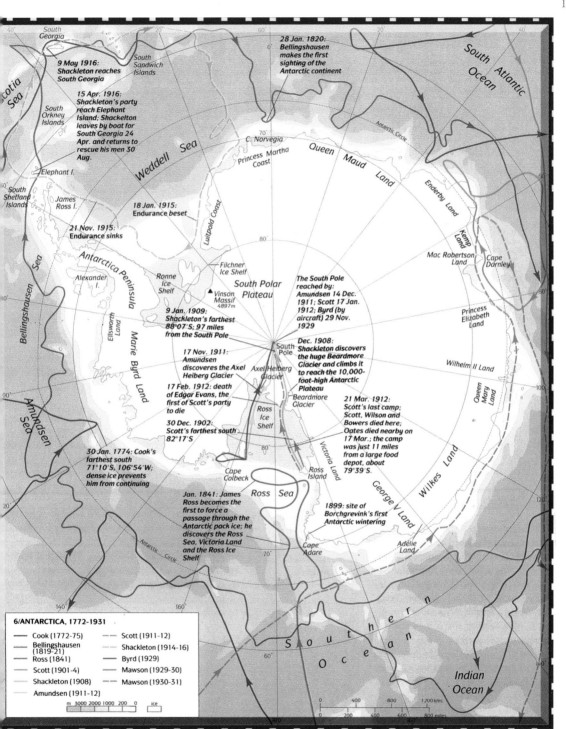

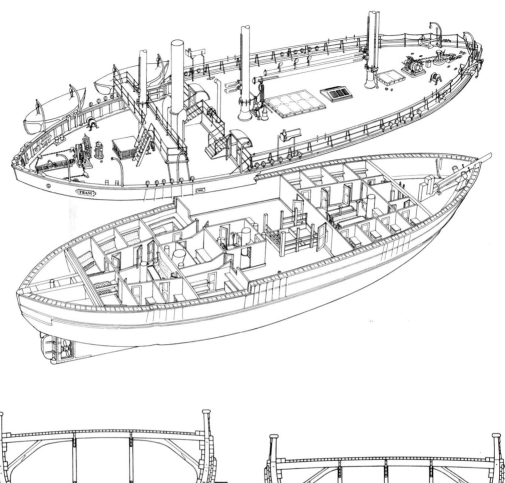

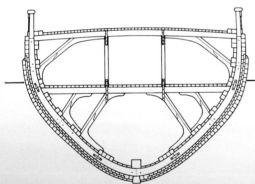

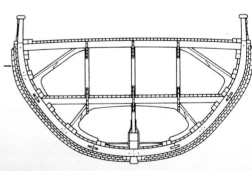

Fram was specially designed to withstand the pressure of pack ice

Fram ble spesialkonstruert for å tåle presset fra ismassenene

Die Fram wurde eigens dafür gebaut, um dem Druck der Eismassen Stand halten zu können.

The building of the Fram

The polar exploration vessel Fram was built to satisfy Fridtjof Nansen's keen desire to prove his theories on the currents of the Arctic Ocean. Prolonged studies in the Arctic Ocean had led him to conclude that there had to be a current flowing from a point north of Asia, and perhaps crossing the Pole itself before turning south between Svalbard and Greenland.

His theory was further borne out by the discovery of articles of clothing and other flotsam, which he believed to originate from an ill-starred American expedition that had sailed in the Jeanette. These objects were found on the southwest coast of Greenland, whereas the Jeanette had foundered off the New Siberian Islands in 1881.

Fram blir bygget

Polarskipet Fram er et resultat av Fridtjof Nansens trang til å bevise sine teorier om strømforholdene i Polhavet. Ved sine lange undersøkelser i Nordishavet var han kommet til det resultat at det måtte gå en strøm fra områdene nord for Asia, kanskje over selve Nordpolen og sydover mellom Svalbard og Grønland.

Teorien hans bygde på en rekke observasjoner, bl.a. klesartikler og annet som han antok stammet fra den amerikanske ekspedisjon Jeanette. Disse ble funnet på Grønlands sydvestkyst mens Jeanette forliste ved Ny-Sibirøyene i 1881.

Nansen møtte stor motstand fra utenlandske vitenskapsmenn, men han fikk tilslutning av Det Norske Geografiske Selskab da han fremla sin teori den

Der Bau der Fram

Das Polarschiff Fram wurde zum Beweis der Richtigkeit von Fridtjof Nansens Theorien über die Strömungsverhältnisse im nördlichen Polarmeer gebaut. Anhand eingehender Studien im nördlichen Polarmeer war er zu dem Ergebnis gekommen, dass es eine Strömung geben musste, die sich aus den nördlich von Asien gelegenen Gebieten, vielleicht sogar über den Nordpol, in südliche Richtung zwischen Spitzbergen und Grönland bewegt.

Seine Theorie stützte sich auf eine Reihe von Beobachtungen, u.a. dem Fund von Kleidungsstücken und anderen Dingen, die, wie er annahm, von der amerikanischen Expedition Jeanette stammten und an der

Fram on its slipway 1892   Fram på beddingen 1892   Fram auf der Helling 1892

Fram is launched 1892   Fram er sjøsatt 1892   Fram läuft vom Stapel 1892

Nansen's theories were met with fierce opposition from scientists abroad, but he received support from the Norwegian Geographical Society when he presented his theory on February 18th 1890.

He wished to substantiate his claims by building a small ship sturdy enough to drift in the grip of the ice, with a handpicked crew on board, clear across the Arctic Ocean without being crushed or breaking up. It is to Fridtjof Nansen's bold theories that the Fram owes her novel design and proportions. Today, the Fram occupies a unique position in the history of exploration as the only ship in the world to have sailed so far north and south.

After the Norwegian Storting (National Assembly) had made a grant of NOK 280,000 available for the venture and various enthusiastic private citizens had added their contributions, the work of building a polar exploration vessel to Nansen's specifications commenced.

Nansen's closest adviser on the project was Otto Sverdrup, while the building work was entrusted to Colin Archer. It was a formidable task. Nansen wanted a ship which, though small and light, would be strong enough to withstand the tremendous pressure of the pack ice, a

18. februar 1890.

Han ville bevise sine påstander ved å bygge et lite skip som med et utvalgt mannskap kunne la seg drive med isen over Polhavet uten å bli brutt ned. Ut fra Fridtjof Nansens dristige teorier fikk Fram sin spesielle konstruksjon og dimensjonering. I dag inntar Fram en særstilling i vår skipsfarts historie som det skip i verden som har kommet lengst mot nord og lengst mot syd.

Etter at Stortinget hadde bevilget 280 000 kr. og en rekke entusiaster hadde gitt sitt bidrag til en polarskute etter Nansens ideer, ble byggingen av Fram satt ut i livet.

Otto Sverdrup var Nansens nære rådgiver, og Colin Archer påtok seg byggingen av skipet. Dette var en uhyre komplisert oppgave. Nansen ville ha et skip som var så lite og lett som mulig. Samtidig skulle det være så solid at det tålte skruisens enorme press, ha en slik form at det ble løftet opp av isen og ikke presset ned, og endelig skulle det være et trivelig oppholdssted for mannskapet som måtte være innstilt på å tilbringe flere år om bord. Det endelige resultatet ble et betydelig større skip enn Nansen hadde tenkt seg, nemlig med et deplasement på 800 tonn, lengde ca. 39 m., bredde ca. 11 m. og dyptgående ca. 5 m.

Südwestküste Grönlands gefunden wurden, nachdem die Jeanette 1881 bei den Neusibirischen Inseln unterging.

Ausländische Wissenschaftler begegneten den Theorien Nansens mit großer Skepsis. Als er sie aber am 18. Februar 1890 der Norwegischen Geographischen Gesellschaft vorlegte, fand er dort Unterstützung.

Er wollte beweisen, dass seine Behauptungen stimmten und ließ ein kleines Schiff bauen, das sich – mit einer sorgfältig ausgewählten Mannschaft bemannt – mit dem Eis über das Polarmeer treiben lassen konnte, ohne von diesem zermalmt zu werden. Fridtjof Nansens kühne Theorien bilden die Grundlage der speziellen Konstruktion und Dimensionierung der Fram, die in der Geschichte unserer Seefahrt ein Kleinod darstellt, ist sie doch das Schiff, das am weitesten gegen Norden und gegen Süden vorgedrungen ist.

Nachdem vom Storting (dem norwegischen Parlament) 280.000 Kronen bewilligt wurden und eine Reihe begeisterter Gönner Beiträge für ein Polarschiff nach Nansens Ideen geleistet hatten, wurde mit dem Bau der Fram begonnen.

Otto Sverdrup war

ship with a hull designed to ensure that it would be lifted up by the ice and not forced under and churned to pieces; moreover, it had to provide a comfortable home for the crew, who would have to be prepared to spend several years on board. In the event, the ship proved bigger than Nansen had envisaged: it had a displacement of 800 tons, measured some 39 metres from stem to stern, was 11 metres in the beam, and had a draught of 5 metres. On June 3rd 1893 the Fram was ready to put to sea.

Three times the skill of the designer and shipwrights, combined with first-class navigation and outstanding seamanship, brought the Fram safely home from hazardous voyages in uncharted waters. Today, this proud little ship is on display for all to admire in the museum at Bygdøy, Oslo that bears her name.

Den 3. juni 1893 lå Fram klar til å seile.

Takket være riktige beregninger, dyktig skipsbyggerkunst og fremragende sjømannskap, løste Fram sin oppgave gjennom tre farefulle ferder i ukjent farvann og ligger i dag vel forvart i Frammuseet på Bygdøy, hvor vi kan fryde oss over den stolte skuta.

Nansens engster Berater, und der Bau des Schiffes wurde Colin Archer anvertraut. Es war eine äußerst komplizierte Aufgabe. Nansen wollte ein möglichst kleines und leichtes Schiff haben, doch sollte es so solide sein, dass es den enormen Anforderungen des Packeises standhielt. Durch seine Form sollte es sich vom Eis anheben und nicht niederdrücken lassen. Der Aufenthalt an Bord sollte außerdem behaglich sein für die Mannschaft, die darauf vorbereitet sein musste, mehrere Jahre an Bord zu verbringen. Das Schiff wurde dann doch bedeutend größer als Nansen gedacht hatte: Es erhielt nämlich ein Deplacement von 800 Tonnen, eine Länge von ca. 39 m, eine Breite von ca. 11 m und einen Tiefgang von ca. 5 m. Am 3. Juni 1893 war die Fram seeklar.

Dank richtiger Berechnungen, tüchtiger Schiffsbaukunst und hervorragender Seemannschaft hat die Fram ihren Auftrag auf gefahrvollen Seefahrten in unbekannten Gewässern erfüllt und liegt heute gut verwahrt im Fram Museum in Bygdøy, wo wir das stolze Schiff bewundern können.

Deltagere:

Fridtjof Nansen
Otto Sverdrup
Sigurd Scott Hansen
Henrik Greve Blessing
Theodor C. Jacobsen
Anton Amundsen
Adolf Juell
Lars Pettersen
F. Hjalmar Johansen
Peder L. Hendriksen
Bernhard Nordahl
Ivar O. Mogstad
Bernt Bentsen

The first Fram expedition

On June 24th 1893 the Fram set out on her first expedition. Fridtjof Nansen was in charge of the scientific side and Otto Knoph Neumann Sverdrup captained the ship.

The voyage along the rugged coast of Norway proved a touching farewell with her homeland. The Fram and her crew were given a rousing send-off, not only at her ports of call, but also in countless hamlets and fishing villages along the coast, as well as by the ships she met en route.

On July 21st of that year the Fram left Vardø, on the north coast of Norway, bound for the New Siberian Islands, and by September 22nd she had reached the ice. Her subsequent drift across the Arctic Ocean confirmed

Frams første ekspedisjon

Den 24. juni 1893 la Fram ut på sin første ekspedisjon med Fridtjof Nansen som leder og Otto Knoph Neumann Sverdrup som fører.

Reisen langs Norges kyst ble en rørende avskjed med fedrelandet. Ikke bare i byene Fram anløp, men fra bosteder langs kysten og fra farkoster de møtte, lød jublende tilrop.

Den 21. juli 1893 stevnet Fram ut fra Vardø med kurs for Ny-Sibirøyene og frøs fast i isen den 22. september. Driften over Polhavet ble en klar bekreftelse på at Nansens teori var riktig idet Fram drev mellom Nordpolen og Frans Josef land. Turen tok vel tre år, og mange ganger endret kursen seg slik at det så ut som Fram var kommet inn i bakevjer i strømmen. Fram

Die erste Expedition der Fram

Am 24. Juni 1893 trat die Fram ihre erste Expedition mit Fridtjof Nansen als Leiter und Otto Knoph Neumann Sverdrup als Schiffsführer an.

Die Reise entlang der norwegischen Küste war ein rührender Abschied vom Heimatland. Nicht nur in den Städten, die die Fram anlief, sondern von überall her, auch von begegnenden Fahrzeugen, erschallten jubelnde Zurufe.

Am 21. Juli 1893 verließ die Fram Vardø mit Kurs auf die Neusibirischen Inseln, und am 22. September war das Schiff im Eis eingefroren. Die Abdrift über das Polarmeer bestätigte die Richtigkeit der Theorie von Nansen. Denn die Fram trieb mit dem Eis zwischen dem Nordpol und Franz-Josef-Land. Die

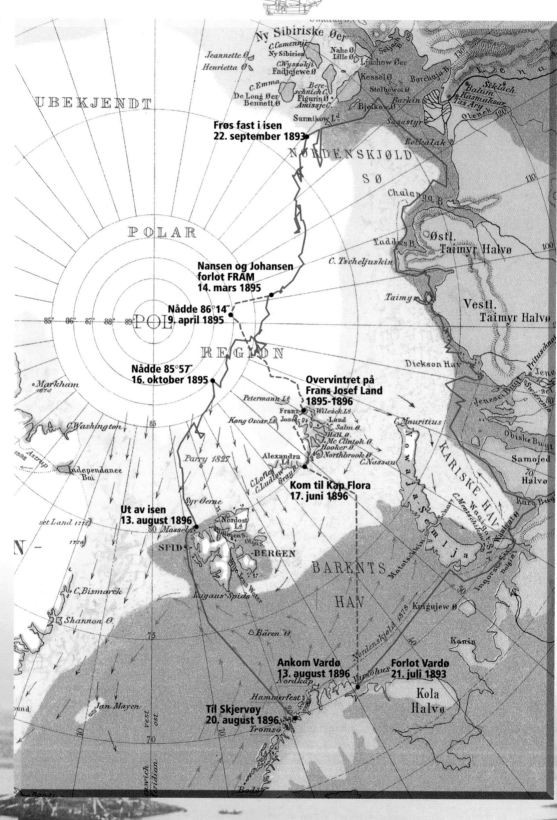

UBEKJENDT

POLAR

POL

REGION

Ny Sibiriske Øer

**Frøs fast i isen
22. september 1893**

**Nansen og Johansen
forlot FRAM
14. mars 1895**

**Nådde 86°14´
9. april 1895**

**Nådde 85°57´
16. oktober 1895**

**Overvintret på
Frans Josef Land
1895-1896**

**Kom til Kap Flora
17. juni 1896**

**Ut av isen
13. august 1896**

**Ankom Vardø
13. august 1896**

**Forlot Vardø
21. juli 1893**

**Til Skjervøy
20. august 1896**

NORDENSKJØLD
SØ

Taimyr Halvø

Vestl.
Taimyr Halvø

Dickson Hav

KARISKE HAV

BARENTS
HAV

Kola
Halvø

Jan Mayen

SPIDS-

BERGEN

Nansen's theory to the hilt, locked in the ice, the Fram was carried for hundreds of miles between the North Pole and Franz Josef Land. The voyage took just over three years, and the course of her drift changed many times, leading those on board to fear that they were trapped in eddies or backwaters of the main current. Nor did they get as close to the Pole as Nansen had hoped - the northernmost point reached was 85° 57' N, where they found themselves on October 16th 1895. There is reason to believe, however, that the Fram would have drifted closer to the Pole if the expedition had succeeded in penetrating further north before running into the ice barrier in the autumn of 1893.

When Nansen realised that the Fram would not get as close to the North Pole as he had expected, he and Hjalmar Johansen left the ship on March 14th 1895 and set out with three dog-drawn sledges in a bold bid to make the Pole across the ice. But the pack ice was in constant motion and they were compelled to abandon the attempt on April 9th, by which time they had reached 86° 14' N. They then set course for Franz Josef land, where they built a crude hut in which they were forced to spend the winter. In May

kom heller ikke så nær Nordpolen som Nansen hadde håpet. Den nordligste posisjon ble notert den 16. oktober 1895 på 85 gr. 57 min. nordlig bredde. Man har imidlertid grunn til å tro at Fram ville ha drevet nærmere Nordpolen hvis fartøyet var kommet lenger mot nord før det møtte isen høsten 1893.

Da det ble klart for Nansen at Fram ikke ville komme så nær Nordpolen som han hadde forutsatt, forlot han og Hjalmar Johansen skipet den 14. mars 1895 med tre sleder og hunder, for å prøve å ta seg frem til Nordpolen over isen. På grunn av store bevegelser i isen måtte de gi opp forsøket etter å ha nådd frem til 86 gr. 14 min. nordlig bredde den 9. april. Herfra satte de kurs mot Frans Josef land. Her bygde de en hytte og måtte overvintre. I mai 1896 forlot de hytta, og i to sammenbundet kajakker dro de langs kysten og nådde Kap Flora den 17. juni s.å. Ved et merkelig sammentreff møtte Nansen engelskmannen Jackson, som tok de to nordmennene tilbake til Norge om bord i sitt skip Windward. Den 13. august 1896 nådde de Vardø. Nansens beretning om denne reisen av to menn alene i isødet er noe av det mest dramatiske i norsk polarforsknings historie.

Fram med resten av be-

Eismeerfahrt dauerte über 3 Jahre, und oft änderte sich der Kurs dermaßen, dass die Fram in Strömungswirbel oder Stauwasser geriet. Sie bewegte sich auch nicht so nahe am Nordpol vorbei, wie Nansen gehofft hatte. Die nördlichste Position wurde am 16. Oktober 1895 auf 85° 57' n.B. notiert. Es besteht jedoch Grund anzunehmen, dass die Fram sich dem Nordpol noch mehr genähert hätte, wenn sie weiter gegen Norden getrieben wäre, bevor sie im Herbst 1893 auf Eis stieß.

Als Nansen begriff, dass die Fram nicht so nahe wie erwartet an den Nordpol herankommen würde, verließ er das Schiff am 14. März 1895 mit Hjalmar Johansen, 3 Schlitten und Hunden in der Absicht, über das Eis zum Nordpol vorzudringen. Wegen großer Eisbewegungen mussten sie den Versuch aufgeben, und nachdem sie am 9. April den Punkt 86° 14' n.B. erreicht hatten, nahmen sie Kurs auf Franz-Josef-Land. Hier bauten sie sich eine Hütte und mussten überwintern. Im Mai 1896 brachen sie mit zwei zusammengebundenen Kajaks auf, zogen die Küste entlang und erreichten am 17. Juni Kap Flora. Durch einen merkwürdigen Zufall begegnete Nansen dem

Fram locked in the dramatic pack ice in January 1895.

Fram etter den dramatiske isskruingen i januar 1895.

Fram nach dem dramatischen Packeis im Januar 1895.

Nansen and Johansen depart from Fram 14th March 1895

Nansen og Johansen forlater Fram 14. mars 1895

Nansen und Johansen verlassen die Fram am 14. März 1895

Fridtjof Nansen and Hjalmar Johansen paddle across the Polar Sea.

Fridtjof Nansen og Hjalmar Johansen padler over Polhavet.

Fridtjof Nansen und Hjalmar Johansen paddeln über das Polarmeer.

1896 they left their shelter and in two lashed together kayaks made their way along the coast, reaching Cape Flora on June 17th. There, by a remarkable coincidence, they met the British explorer F. G. Jackson, who took them back to Norway on board his ship the Windward. By August 13th 1896 they were back in Vardø. Nansen's account of the journey he and his companion made across the desolate wastes of ice is one of the most dramatic narratives in the annals of Norwegian polar exploration.

Fram, with the rest of her crew, continued to drift west-

setningen fortsatte sin drift vestover langs 85. breddegrad til februar 1896 og drev så av i sørlig retning.

I sin drift over Polhavet ble Fram, som antatt, utsatt for de største påkjenninger med store mengder drivis som presset seg innover dekket. Situasjonen var så kritisk i januar 1895 at utstyr og forråd ble brakt i sikkerhet ute på isen, og mannskapet var forberedt på å forlate skipet. Konstruktørens beregninger holdt imidlertid stikk, og skipet ble løftet opp av isens press. Fram kom ut av isen ved Danskeøya den 13. august 1896, og under ledelse

Engländer Jackson, der die beiden Norweger an Bord seines Schiffes Windward nach Norwegen mitnahm. Am. 13. August 1896 gelangten sie nach Vardø. Nansens Bericht über die Reise von zwei Männer, die alleine in der Eiswüste waren, gehört zu den dramatischsten Erzählungen aus der Geschichte norwegischer Polarforschung.

Die Fram trieb mit der übrigen Besatzung am 85. Breitengrad westwärts weiter und im Februar 1896 trieb sie in Richtung Süden ab.

Während sie durch das Polarmeer trieb, wurde die

wards along the 85th parallel right up to February 1896, when the current turned her southwards.

As Nansen had so rightly foreseen, during the long drift across the Arctic Ocean the ship was subjected to tremendous strain and pressure as vast blocks of pack ice churned and thrust their way onto the deck. In January 1895 the situation became so critical that stores and equipment had to be carried quickly to safety on the ice and the crew prepared to abandon ship. But the builder's faith in his design proved justified, and the Fram was gradually eased upwards, out of the crushing grip of the pack. She finally emerged from the ice off the north coast of West Svalbard on August 13th 1896, the same day that Nansen arrived in Vardø, and on August 20th Captain Sverdrup brought his ship safely to anchor in the harbour of Skjervøy on the northwest coast of Norway.

On September 9th the Fram returned in triumph to her port of departure, Oslo, bringing with her a wealth of valuable scientific material from regions of the earth never before visited by man.

av kaptein Sverdrup, løp fartøyet inn i havnen på Skjervøy den 20. august.

Den 9. september holdt de sitt inntog i Oslo. Fram kom hjem fra sin ferd med et stort vitenskapelig materiale fra en del av vår klode hvor ingen hadde vært før.

Fram – wie erwartet – den ungeheuren Kräften des Treibeises ausgesetzt, das sich über das Deck hinwegwälzte. Im Januar 1895 war die Situation so kritisch, dass Ausrüstung und Vorräte draußen auf dem Eis in Sicherheit gebracht wurden und die Mannschaft darauf vorbereitet war, das Schiff zu verlassen. Die Berechnungen erwiesen sich jedoch als zuverlässig, und das Schiff wurde durch den Druck des Eises hochgehoben. Am 13. August 1896 kam die Fram bei der Däneninsel aus dem Eis heraus, und am 20. August lief sie unter Leitung des Kapitäns Sverdrup in den Hafen von Skjervøy, Nordnorwegen, ein.

Am 9. September hielt das Schiff seinen Einzug in Oslo. Die Fram kam von ihrer Reise mit wertvollem, wissenschaftlichem Material aus Regionen unserer Erde zurück, die vorher noch von keinem Menschen betreten worden waren.

Diner du 9. Septembre 1896.

Potage tortue clair

Lunch à l'Impériale

Brissotins de volaille au suprême

Elies, Sce Norvégienne

Selle de renne piquée, Légumes

Filets de poulets à la Périgord

Pain d'Ecrevisses à la Dartois

Poules de neige rôties, Salade

Fonds d'Artichauts à la Lyonnaise

Pouding à la Montreuil

Fromage, Beurre, Cakes

DESSERT

Glaces Assorties

Compote, petits gâteaux

Fruits

Bonbons

King Oscar II's banquet upon their return

Kong Oscar IIs middag ved hjemkomsten

Mahl bei König Oscar II nach der Heimkehr

2. FRAMFERD 1898-1902

Deltagere:

Otto Sverdrup
Victor Baumann
Oluf Raanes
Gunerius I. Isachsen
Herman G. Simmons
Edvard Bay
Johan Svendsen †
Per Schei

Peder I. Henriksen
Karl Olsen
Jacob Nødtedt
Ivar Fosheim
Adolf H. Lindstrøm
Sverre Hassel
Rudolf Stolz
Ove Braskerud †

The Sverdrup expedition

The Fram's first successful voyage across the Arctic Ocean gave rise to a wave of popular enthusiasm and stimulated the interest of the Norwegian people in polar exploration. This was evidently a field in which Norway could make her mark, and the Norwegians felt themselves better suited to take up the challenge of the North than any of their neighbours. Accordingly, it was soon decided that the time had come to equip the Fram for a new voyage into the unknown. Otto Sverdrup, who had captained the ship on her first voyage, was urged to lead the second expedition. He had already proved his fitness for the task, not only on the

Sverdrups ekspedisjon

Etter Frams første vellykte ferd over Polhavet fulgte en bølge av begeistring, og interessen for norsk polarforskning grep om seg i det norske folk. Norge hadde funnet et område å hevde seg på hvor vi følte at vi stod bedre rustet enn noen av våre naboland. Det ble derfor snart bestemt at Fram måtte utrustes til en ny ferd.

Frams fører på den første ekspedisjonen, Otto Sverdrup ble oppfordret til å lede ferden. Han hadde allerede bevist sin dyktighet, ikke bare på Framferden, men også som Nansens følgesvenn på skituren over Grønlands innlandsis i 1888.

Frams første ferd hadde vist at skipet kunne bli enda bedre

Die Sverdrup Expedition

Nach der ersten erfolgreichen Reise der Fram durch das Polarmeer folgte eine Welle der Begeisterung, die bei den Norwegern das Interesse für Polarforschung weckte. Das war offenbar ein Gebiet, auf dem Norwegen meinte, sich behaupten zu können, und man ging davon aus, dass Norwegen bessere Voraussetzungen hatte als die Nachbarländer. Daher wurde bald der Beschluss gefasst, die Fram für eine neue Reise auszurüsten.

Otto N. Sverdrup, der die Fram schon auf ihrer ersten Expedition geführt hatte, wurde aufgefordert, die Reise zu leiten. Seine Tüchtigkeit hatte er bereits bewiesen, nicht nur während der Fram-

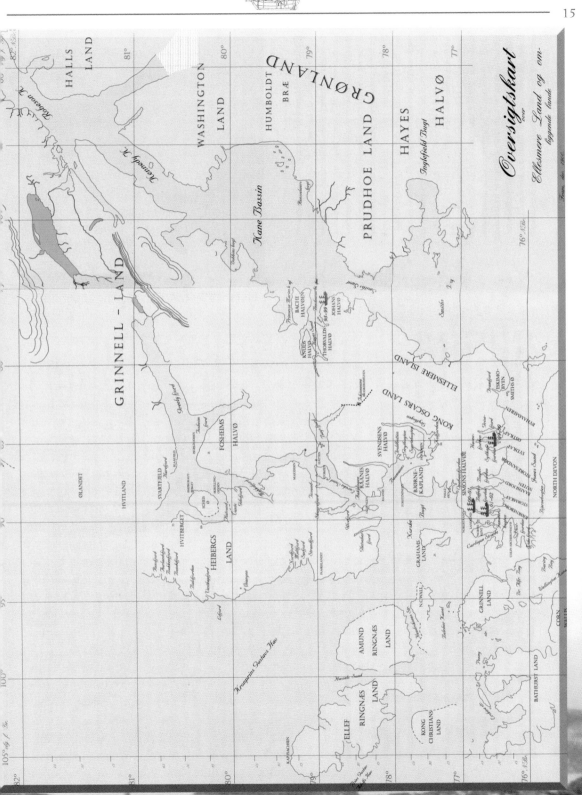

HALLS LAND

81°

WASHINGTON LAND

80°

HUMBOLDT BRÆ

GRØNLAND

79°

PRUDHOE LAND

78°

HAYES HALVØ

77°

Oversigtskart
over
Ellesmere Land og om-
liggende lande

Fram, 1906.

82° Vfl f N.

Robeson K.

Kennedy K.

Kane Bassin

GRINNELL – LAND

ELLESMERE ISLAND

KONG OSCARS LAND

Inglefield Bugt

76° V f N.

Smiths S d

Greely fjord

FOSHEIMS HALVØ

BACHE HALVØEN

KNUDS HALVØ

THORVALDS HALVØ

JOHANS HALVØ

SVENDSENS HALVØ

BJØRNE-KAPLAND

EIDE RNÆS HALVØ

ØLANDET

HVITLAND

SVARTFJELD

HVITBERGET

HEIBERGS LAND

SKREIS

SIMONS HALVØ

GRAHAMS LAND

NORTH DEVON

Kronprins Gustavs Hav

AMUND RINGNÆS LAND

GRINNELL LAND

Cardigan Str.

Hassels Sund

ELLEF RINGNÆS LAND

KONG CHRISTIANS LAND

BATHURST LAND

81°

80°

79°

78°

77°

76° V f N.

105° øf / Gr.

100°

95°

90°

Fram's maiden voyage, but also when he and Nansen had crossed the Greenland ice sheet on skis in 1888.

One of the lessons learned from the Fram's first voyage was that a few alterations would improve the ship even more. Sverdrup therefore raised the freeboard by six feet and built a new deck extending forward from the engine room, thus providing six extra cabins in the forepart of the ship. A false keel was also added to improve lateral stability.

On Midsummer's Day 1898 the Fram was again ready for sea. The mission was to survey Northern Greenland and to explore the eastern coast of Greenland to survey unknown parts of the territory. The second Fram expedition was the most scientific, and included a cartographer, a zoologist, a botanist and a geologist. The expedition was supposed to last for three years. However, it lasted four years because they got trapped by the ice in Gåsefjord. This caused a lot of anxiety at home. Sverdrup did not succeed in pushing his way through Northern Greenland. He started by surveying unknown parts of Ellesmere Island. Amund Ringnes Island, Ellef Ringnes Island and Axel Heiberg Island were also discovered and surveyed. In all

med en del ombygging. Sverdrup økte fribordet med seks fot og bygde et nytt dekk fra maskinrommet og forover, og man fikk seks lugarer til forut. Det ble også bygd på en stråkjøl (falsk kjøl) for å bedre styringen av skipet.

St.Hansdagen 1898 lå Fram igjen seilklar. Oppdraget var å kartlegge Nord Grønland og ta seg over på Grønlands østkyst for å kartlegge ukjente deler av landet. Den 2. Framferden er den mest vitenskaplige, og om bord var det kartograf, zoolog, botaniker og geolog. Ferden skulle vare i tre år. På grunn av at de frøs inne i Gåsefjorden varte ferden i fire år, noe som skapte stor engstelse hjemme. Sverdrup lyktes ikke å trenge gjennom Nord Grønland. Han startet med å kartlegge ukjente deler av Ellesmere Island. Amund og Ellef Rignes-øyene og Axel Heibergs Land ble oppdaget og kartlagt. I alt ble ca. 200 000 kvadratkilometer ukjent land kartlagt, et areal som tilsvarer Syd Norge. Flere hundre norske navn ble satt på fjell, fjorder og land. Områdene ble «taget i den norske Konges navn» av Sverdrup. Siden Storting og Regjering ikke fulgte opp ble områdene overført til Canada i 1930.

Ekspedisjonen kom hjem 18. september 1902. 16 menn

Reise, sondern auch 1888 als Nansens Gefährte auf der Skitour über Grönlands Inlandeis.

Die erste Reise der Fram hatte gezeigt, dass ein kleiner Umbau das Schiff verbessern könnte. Sverdrup vergrößerte das Freibord um 6 Fuß und baute ein neues Deck vom Maschinenraum aus und weiter nach vorne, und so erhielt man sechs neue Kabinen. Außerdem baute man ein Loskiel, um das Schiff manövrierfähiger zu machen.

Am 24. Juni 1898 war die Fram wieder seeklar. Diesmal nahm sie Kurs auf die Nordwestküste von Grönland, wo unbekannte Teile erforscht und kartiert werden sollten. Die zweite Fahrt der Fram war die wissenschaftlichste. An Bord befanden sich ein Kartograph, ein Zoologe, ein Botaniker und ein Geologe. Die Reise sollte drei Jahre dauern. Die Reise wurde jedoch um ein Jahr verlängert, als der Gåsefjord zufror – und zu Hause bangte man sehr. Es gelang Sverdrup nicht, durch Nordgrönland durchzudringen. Er begann unbekannte Teile der Ellesmere Insel zu kartieren. Man entdeckte und kartierte die Ellef Rignes-Inseln sowie Axel Heibergs Land. Es wurden insgesamt 200.000 Quadratkilometer kartiert, d.h. eine Fläche so groß wie

1. Braskerudflya 1899
2. Start of the long journey, April 1901
3. 17th May 1899 (Norwegian Constitution Day)
4. Braskerud's grave
5. The expedition members

1. Braskerudflya 1899
2. Start for langtur, April 1901
3. 17. mai 1899
4. Braskeruds grav
5. Deltagerne på ferden

1. Braskerudflya 1899
2. Vor Antritt der langen Reise, April 1901
3. 17. Mai 1899 (Tag des norwegischen Grundgesetzes)
4. Braskeruds Grab
5. Teilnehmer der Reise

an area of 200,000 square kilometres was surveyed, an area equal to Southern Norway. The land was «claimed in the name of the King of Norway» by Sverdrup. However, since the Norwegian parliament and government neglected to follow this up the land were transferred to Canada in 1930.

The expedition returned home on 18th September 1902. 16 men had set out. The doctor, Johan Svendsen, and Ove Braskerud died during the expedition. Only 14 men returned.

The scientific results were sensational. Thousands of plant samples, 2,000 glass containers of smaller animals, large quantities of plankton, rock and fossil varieties, data about the ice, temperature, the earth's magnetism, and data related to other scientific fields meant that it was many years before the results of the expedition were scientifically processed. In 1919 four volumes were published. An additional volume was published in 1930. All in all the works contained 39 theses.

hadde reist ut. Legen Johan Svendsen og Ove Braskerud døde under ekspedisjonen. Bare 14 menn vendte tilbake. De vitenskaplige resultatene var oppsiktsvekkende. Tusenvis av planteprøver, 2000 glass med lavere dyr, store mengder plankton, bergarter og fossiler, data om is, temperatur, jordmagnetisme og data innen andre vitenskaplige felter mange år før resultatene var vitenskaplig bearbeidet. Det kom ut fire bind i 1919 og et tilleggsbind i 1930. Verket inneholdt i alt 39 avhandlinger.

Südnorwegen. Berge, Fjorde und Gebiete erhielten mehrere hundert norwegische Namen. Sverdrup nahm die Gebiete «im Namen des norwegischen Königs» ein. Da das norwegische Parlament, das Storting, und die Regierung die Gebiete jedoch nicht nachhaltig beanspruchten, wurden sie 1930 an Kanada übergeben.

Am 18. September 1902 erreichte die Expedition wieder die Heimat. 16 Mann hatten an der Expedition teilgenommen, aber nur 14 kehrten zurück. Der Arzt Johan Svendsen sowie Ove Braskerud starben auf der Reise.

Die wissenschaftlichen Ergebnisse erregten großes Aufsehen. Tausende von Pflanzenproben, 2000 Gläser mit niederen Tieren, große Mengen Plankton, Bergarten und Fossilien, Notizen über Eis, Temperatur, Erdmagnetismus sowie Notizen auf anderen wissenschaftlichen Gebieten – so viel Material, dass es viele Jahre dauerte, bevor alles wissenschaftlich ausgewertet werden konnte. Vier Bände wurden veröffentlicht 1919 und ein Zusatzband 1930. Insgesamt beinhalteten die Bücher 39 Abhandlungen.

Deltagere:
Roald Amundsen
Thorvald Nilsen
Olav Bjaaland
Helmer Hanssen
Sverre Hassel
Oscar Wisting
Andreas Beck
Hjalmar Fredrik Gjertsen
Ludvig Hansen
Fredrik Hjalmar Johansen
Henrik Adolf Lindstrøm
Jacob Nødtvedt
Karenius Olsen

Halvardus Kristensen
Kristian Presterud
Martin Rønne
Jørgen Stubberud
Knut Sundbeck
Alexandr Kutschin

Buenos Aires:
Avmønstret 1911
Alexandr Kutschin

Påmønstret 1911
A. Olsen
F. Steller

The Antarctic

On her safe return from the Sverdrup expedition, the Fram was laid up at the naval base in Horten. It was doubted for a long time whether she would ever again be used for the purpose for which she had been built, and at one time there were even plans to convert the ship into a museum.

Roald Amundsen had plans of a different kind however, he was considering drifting across the Arctic Ocean, as Nansen had done. He thought however, that if he were to sail through the Bering Strait, it would give him a better starting point and improve his chances of getting close to the Pole.

In the meantime, the American explorer Robert E.

Til Sydpolen

Da Fram var kommet vel i havn etter Sverdrups ekspedisjon, gikk skuta i opplag ved Marinestasjonen i Horten. Det var lenge uvisst om det ville bli bruk for Fram på flere ferder, og ideen om å bruke polarskuten til museum dukket opp.

Roald Amundsen gikk imidlertid med planer om å la seg drive over Polhavet slik Nansen allerede hadde gjort, men mente at ved å seile gjennom Beringstredet, ville han ha en gunstigere utgangsposisjon og dermed ha mulighet for å komme nærmere Nordpolen.

I mellomtiden ble det kjent at amerikaneren Robert E. Peary gjorde krav på å ha nådd Nordpolen den 6. april 1909. Derfor fikk Amundsen

Zum Südpol

Nach Sverdrups Expedition wohlbehalten in der Heimat angekommen, wurde die Fram in der Marinestation in Horten aufgelegt. Es war lange ungewiss, ob man sie noch für weitere Fahrten verwenden würde, weshalb der Gedanke auftauchte, sie in ein Museum zu bringen.

Roald Amundsen hatte jedoch andere Pläne. Er wollte sich so wie Nansen übers Polarmeer treiben lassen, meinte aber, dass die Startposition günstiger wäre, wenn er durch die Beringstrasse segelte, was auch seine Chancen, dem Nordpol näher zu kommen erhöhen sollte.

Inzwischen war bekannt geworden, dass der Amerikaner Robert E. Peary den Anspruch erhob, am 6.

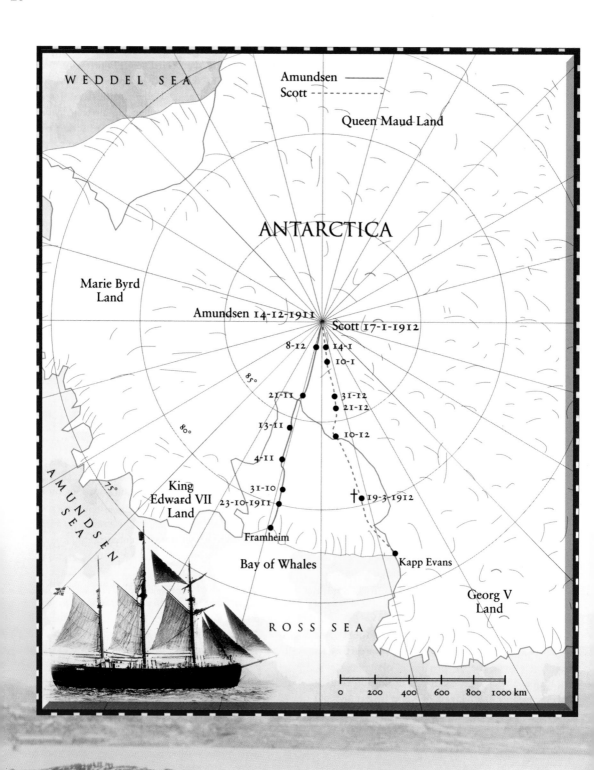

WEDDEL SEA

Amundsen ————
Scott - - - - - -

Queen Maud Land

ANTARCTICA

Marie Byrd
Land

Amundsen 14-12-1911   Scott 17-1-1912

8-12   14-1
10-1

85°

21-11   31-12
21-12

13-11   10-12

80°

4-11

King
Edward VII   31-10
Land   23-10-1911

✝ 19-3-1912

75°

A
M
U
N
D
S
E
N

Framheim

Kapp Evans

Bay of Whales

Georg V
Land

ROSS SEA

0   200   400   600   800   1000 km

Peary's claim to have reached the North Pole on April 6th 1909 was announced. This news fired Amundsen with a desire to make a bid for the South Pole as well, as he would in any case have to sail a long way south in order to round Cape Horn. He took great pains to keep this decision a secret, even from his crew, which meant that he had to do all the detailed planning himself.

The Fram left Kristiansand on her third voyage of exploration on August 10th 1910. When she put in at Funchal, on the island of Madeira, Amundsen informed the crew of the change in plan, a piece of news they received with enthusiasm. The expedition then set course for the Ross Sea, anchoring in the Bay of Whales on January 14th 1911.

The British explorer Robert Falcon Scott had put to sea with his ship the Terra Nova on June 15th 1910 he too was bound for the South Pole. When he arrived in Melbourne on October 12th, Scott found awaiting him a telegram from Madeira. It was brief and to the point: «Beg leave to inform you. Fram proceeding Antarctic Amundsen.»

Amundsen divided his expedition into two parties. One party, comprising ten men under Captain Thorvald

lyst til å forsøke å nå Sydpolen på sin reise som allikevel måtte gå så langt mot syd som rundt Kapp Horn. Denne beslutningen ble holdt strengt hemmelig selv for mannskapet, og Roald Amundsen var derfor alene om den nærmere planleggingen.

Fram gikk ut på sin tredje reise fra Kristiansand 10.

The South Pole, 1911
Sydpolen 1911
Der Südpol 1911

august 1910. Ved anløp av Funchal på Madeira, ble mannskapet underrettet om Amundsens endrede planer om at ferden gikk sydover med Sydpolen som mål. Nyheten ble mottatt med begeistring. Fram satte kurs for Rosshavet og ankret opp i Hvalbukten 14. januar 1911.

Engelskmannen Robert Falcon Scott forlot England med sitt skip Terra Nova den 15. juni 1910, også med

April 1909 den Nordpol erreicht zu haben. Da kam Amundsen auf die Idee, auf seiner Reise, die ohnehin so weit gegen Süden wie um das Kap Horn gedacht war, den Südpol zu erreichen zu versuchen. Dieser Plan, von dem nur Roald Amundsen wusste, wurde selbst vor der Mannschaft streng geheimgehalten.

Am 10. August 1910 verließ die Fram Kristiansand und startete somit ihre dritte Entdeckungsfahrt. Bei der Ankunft in Funchal auf der Insel Madeira, wurde die Mannschaft über die neuen Pläne von Amundsen in Kenntnis gesetzt. Dass die Fahrt den Südpol als Ziel hatte, war eine Neuigkeit, die Begeisterung auslöste. Die Fram nahm Kurs auf das Rossmeer, und am 14. Januar 1911 ging sie in der Walfischbucht vor Anker.

Der Engländer Robert Falcon Scott verließ England mit seinem Schiff Terra Nova am 15. Juni 1910, ebenfalls mit dem Südpol als Ziel. Bei der Ankunft in Melbourne, Australien, fand Scott am 12. Oktober ein Telegramm aus Madeira mit folgendem Wortlaut vor: «Beg leave to inform you. Fram proceeding Antarktis. Amundsen.»

Amundsens Expedition wurde in zwei Teile geteilt. Die Seepartie, bestehend aus

Nilsen, was charged with carrying out oceanographic studies in the Antarctic Ocean. On this voyage the Fram reached a latitude of 78° 41' S, the furthest south a ship had ever penetrated.

Sydpolen som mål. Ved ankomsten til Melbourne i Australia den 12. oktober lå det et telegram og ventet på Scott: «Beg leave to inform you. Fram proceeding Antarctic. Amundsen».

10 Mann unter der Leitung des Kapitäns Thv. Nilsen, sollte sich mit ozeanographischen Untersuchungen im Südlichen Eismeer befassen. Die Fram erreichte auf dieser Reise 78° 41' s.B., den süd-

Roald Amundsen at the South Pole

Roald Amundsen på Sydpolen

Roald Amundsen am Südpol

The nine men who made up the other party, the shore party, were split into two groups: one group, under Amundsen, was to aim for the Pole, while the other, comprising three men, was detailed to explore Edward VII Land. Amundsen and his four companions, with their dog teams, reached the South Pole on December 14th 1911. When Scott's party of five reached it on January 17th 1912, it was to find the Norwegian flag firmly planted in the snow. Scott and his four companions perished on the return journey, dying of cold and starvation, only a few

Amundsens ekspedisjon ble delt i to partier. Et sjøparti bestående av 10 menn under ledelse av kaptein Thv. Nilsen, skulle drive oceanografiske undersøkelser i Sydishavet. Fram nådde på denne turen 78 gr. 41 min. sydlig bredde, det sydligste punkt noe skip til da hadde nådd.

Et landparti bestående av 9 menn ble delt i to grupper. En gruppe skulle gjøre fremstøt mot polen. En annen gruppe med tre menn fikk i oppdrag å utforske Edward VIIs Land.

Amundsen med fire menn og hundespann nådde Sydpolen den 14. desember

lichsten Punkt, den ein Schiff je erreicht hatte.

Die Landpartie, bestehend aus 9 Mann, wurde in zwei Gruppen geteilt. Die eine Gruppe sollte zum Südpol vorstoßen. Die andere Gruppe, drei Mann, hatte den Auftrag, das Eduard-VII.-Land zu erforschen.

Amundsen erreichte den Südpol am 14. Dezember 1911 mit vier Begleitern und einem Hundegespann. Scott gelangte am 17. Januar 1912 mit vier Gefährten zum Südpol, wo er die wehende norwegische Flagge vorfand. Auf dem Rückmarsch ist Scott mit seinen vier

miles from a depot -One-Ton Camp - stocked with fuel and provisions.

By January 27th 1912 the Fram was back in the Bay of Whales, where she picked up the other members of the expedition, and on January 31st they sailed clear of the Ice Barrier.

The Fram reached Hobart in Tasmania on March 7th, remaining there until March 20th. When the ship reached Buenos Aires on May 25th, Amundsen was informed that there was a chance of the Fram becoming one of the first ships to sail through the Panama Canal. Accordingly, orders were issued to proceed to Colon, where the ship arrived on October 3rd 1913. On December 1th, as it was still not known for certain when the canal would be opened, the captain was ordered to set course for San Francisco round Cape Horn, it being Amundsen's intention to continue northwards for an attack on the Arctic Ocean. However, one hundred days later, when they reached Buenos Aires, Amundsen countermanded his previous order and told Captain Nilsen to set course for home. The Fram returned to Horten on July 16th 1914.

1911. Scott med fire ledsagere nådde polen den 17. januar 1912, hvor han fant det norske flagg og flaggvimpelen vaiende. På tilbaketuren omkom Scott og hans fire kamerater. De sultet og frøs langsomt ihjel, bare noen få nautiske mil fra depotet One-Ton Camp hvor det lå både proviant og brensel.

Den 27. januar 1912 kom Fram til Hvalbukten og tok ekspedisjonens medlemmer om bord. Den 31. januar forlot de isbarrieren.

7. mars kom Fram til Hobart på Tasmania og ble liggende til 20. mars. De ankom Buenos Aires den 25. mai. Her fikk Amundsen beskjed om at Fram kunne være blant de første skip som skulle få passere gjennom Panamakanalen. Fram ble derfor beordret til Colon og lå der fra 3. oktober 1913 til l. desember s. å. Da de ikke kunne få sikker beskjed om når kanalen ville bli åpnet, fikk Frams fører ordre om å seile sydover rundt Kapp Horn til San Francisco. Amundsens hensikt var nemlig å fortsette i nord til nytt angrep på Polhavet. Da Fram 100 dager senere kom til Buenos Aires, fikk kaptein Nilsen ordre fra Amundsen om å seile hjem. Fram ankom Horten den 16. juli 1914.

Begleitern ums Leben gekommen. Sie sind nach und nach verhungert und erfroren, nur 20 km vom Depot «One-Ton Camp» entfernt, wo Proviant und Brennstoff bereitlagen.

Am 27. Januar 1912 kam die Fram zur Walfischbucht und nahm die Mitglieder der Expedition an Bord. Am 31. Januar verließen sie die Eisbarriere.

Am 7. März traf die Fram in Hobart, Tasmanien, ein, wo sie bis zum 20. März liegen blieb. Am 25. Mai kam sie nach Buenos Aires. Hier wurde Amundsen mitgeteilt, dass die Fram zu den ersten Schiffen gehören konnte, die den Panamakanal durchqueren durften. Die Fram wurde daher nach Colon beordert. Dort lag sie vom 3. Oktober bis 1. Dezember 1913. Da jedoch kein sicherer Bescheid zu erhalten war, wann der Kanal eröffnet werden sollte, erhielt der Kapitän der Fram die Weisung, Kurs südwärts auf San Franzisko um das Kap Horn zu nehmen. Amundsen hatte nämlich feste Pläne für eine neue Reise ins Nordpolarmeer. Als die Fram 100 Tage später nach Buenos Aires kam, gab Amundsen Kapitän Nilsen die Weisung, heimwärts zu segeln. Die Fram traf am 16. Juli 1914 in Horten ein.

GJØA 1903-1906

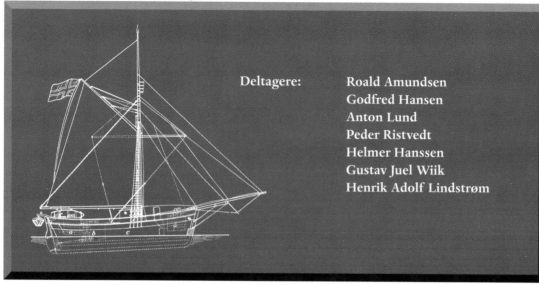

Deltagere:

Roald Amundsen
Godfred Hansen
Anton Lund
Peder Ristvedt
Helmer Hanssen
Gustav Juel Wiik
Henrik Adolf Lindstrøm

Gjøa

Roald Amundsen was still a young man when he made up his mind to be an explorer, and the Polar Regions were what fascinated him most. He had witnessed Fridtjof Nansen's homecoming in 1889, and an idea had taken root - «If only I could master the Northwest Passage!»

His mother, however, had quite different plans -her son was to be a doctor, and out of loyalty to her he set about his medical studies. Following his mother's death, however, he gave up medicine and took his mate's exam instead. He was given a chance to fulfil his boyhood dream when he was engaged as second mate on board the Belgian ship Belgica which, under Adrian de Gerlache's command,

Gjøa

Allerede i ung alder bestemte Roald Amundsen seg for å bli oppdager, og det var de polare områdene han hadde spesielt lyst til å utforske. Han hadde bivånet Fridtjof Nansens hjemkomst i 1889, og tanken slo rot i ham, «Om du kunne gjøre Nordvest Passagen!»

Moren hadde imidlertid ønsker om at sønnen skulle bli lege, og i lojalitet til henne satte han i gang med medisinske studier. Etter morens død ga han opp medisinen og tok istedenfor styrmannseksamen. Han fikk sjansen til å realisere sine ungdomsdrømmer da han fikk jobb som 2. styrmann om bord i det belgiske ekspedisjonsfartøyet Belgica, som under ledelse av Adrian de Gerlache gjennomførte han

Gjøa

Roald Amundsen hatte sich schon als junger Mann dazu entschlossen, Entdecker zu werden, und besonders interessierten ihn die polaren Gebiete. Er hatte 1889 die Heimkehr Fridtjof Nansens erlebt, und von da an war er von einem Gedanken besessen:
«Wenn ich nur die Nordwest-Passage schaffen könnte!»

Seine Mutter hatte allerdings andere Pläne. Der Sohn sollte Arzt werden, und aus reiner Loyalität ihr gegenüber begann er mit dem Medizinstudium. Nach dem Tod der Mutter gab er das Studium auf und erwarb statt dessen das Steuermannspatent. Die Möglichkeit, seine Jugendträume zu verwirklichen, bekam er, als er als 2.

carried out an Antarctic expedition in 1897-1899.

However, the Northwest Passage continued to be the ultimate goal of all his dreams. Numerous attempts to sail the Northwest Passage had so far failed. They had also led to many a tragedy, the most serious being the failure of the Franklin expedition, when the vessels Terror and Erebus disappeared with more than 130 men on board.

Roald Amundsen bought the Hardanger sloop Gjøa with her modest 47 net register tons, and had her fitted with a protective ice hide and a 13 horsepower engine. During the night between 16th and 17th June 1903, the Gjøa set sail for the Arctic seas. Amundsen's initial aim was to locate the magnetic North Pole. To do so, he had been to Germany to acquire the scientific knowledge needed to be able to make the necessary measurements.

He spent two winters in Gjøa Haven, where he became familiar with the local Inuit. They taught him how to build an igloo and how to coat sledge runners with ice to achieve optimal glide. Amundsen gained enormous respect for the way in which the Inuit dressed and for their ability to live in keeping with nature, and not contrary to it. These Inuit were of the

en antarktisk ekspedisjon i 1897-1899.

Det var imidlertid Nordvestpassasjen som var hans drømmers mål. Utallige forsøk på å seile gjennom Nordvestpassasjen hadde vært gjort, men uten heldig resul-tat. Forsøkene hadde også ført til mange tragedier. Den mest alvorlige var Franklin-ekspedisjonens undergang da ekspedisjonsfartøyene Terror og Erebus forsvant med mer enn 130 menn om bord.

Roald Amundsen kjøpte Hardangerjakten Gjøa på beskjedne 47 netto register-tonn, som ble utstyrt med ishud og en motor på 13 hestekrefter. Natt til 17. juni 1903 stevnet Gjøa mot Pol-havet. Amundsens første hensikt var å lokalisere den magnetiske nordpol. Han hadde derfor tilegnet seg spesialutdannelse i Tyskland for å kunne foreta de nødvendige målinger.

To overvintringer fant sted i Gjøahavn. Her ble han kjent med inuitene. Av dem lærte han å bygge iglooer og isbelegge sledemeier for å få

Steuermann auf dem belgi-schen Expeditionsschiff Belgica anheuerte, das 1897-1899 unter der Leitung von Adrian de Gerlache eine Antarktisexpedition durchführte.

Ziel seiner Träume war jedoch die Nordwest-Passage. Unzählige Versuche, die Nordwest-Passage zu durch-queren, waren gescheitert. Diese Versuche endeten mit manch einer Tragödie. Die schrecklichste war der Untergang der Franklin-Expedition, als die Expeditionsschiffe Terror und Erebus mit mehr als 130 Mann an Bord verschwanden.

Roald Amundsen kaufte die mit 47 Nettoregister-tonnen eher bescheidene Hardangerjacht Gjøa, die mit einem Eisgürtel und einem 13 PS starken Motor ausgerüstet wurde. In der Nacht vom 16. auf den 17. Juni 1903 startete die Gjøa in Richtung Polarmeer. Amundsens erstes Ziel war die Lokalisierung des magnetischen Nordpols. Um die dafür nötigen Messungen durchführen zu können, hatte er sich in Deutschland speziell ausbilden lassen.

In Gjøahavn überwinterte das Schiff zweimal. Hier lernte Amundsen die Eskimos kennen. Sie brachten ihm bei, wie Iglus gebaut und Schlittenkufen eisbelegt werden, um deren

Netsilik tribe.

Amundsen bartered away goods in exchange for many Inuit objects. Lindstrøm, the expedition cook, was the one responsible for taking care of these bartered goods, and it is primarily thanks to him that the extensive collection of

ekstra god gli. Amundsen fikk stor respekt inuitenes måte å kle seg på og deres evne til å leve *med* naturen, og ikke *mot* den. Inuitene var av Netsilik-stammen.

Amundsen byttet til seg mange inuitgjenstander. Den som først og fremst tok

Gleitfähigkeit zu erhöhen.

Amundsen wurde stark beeindruckt von der Lebens-weise der Inuitten, wie sie sich kleideten und mit der Natur lebten, anstatt sie nur auszunutzen. Die Inuitten gehörten zum Stamm der Netchilli. Durch Tausch kam

1. Members of the Gjøa expedition
2. Winter in the Gjøa Haven

1. Deltagerne i Gjøa-ferden
2. Vinter i Gjøahavn

1. Teilnehmer an der Gjøa-Reise
2. Winter in Gjøahavn

Inuit artefacts is intact today in the Ethnographic Museum in Oslo.

The experiences Amundsen reaped from the winters he spent here from 1903 to 1905 were invaluable to him, and were probably of decisive significance to his subsequent triumph in 1911, when he was the first man ever to reach the South Pole.

On 26th August 1905 the Northwest Passage was finally breached, and the magnetic North Pole located and chart-

vare på de innbyttede gjenstander var den bekjente polarkokken Lindstrøm. Takket være han er den store samlingen med inuitgjenstan-der nå bevart ved Etnografisk Museum i Oslo.

De erfaringer han gjorde vintrene 1903-1905 ble til stor nytte for Amundsen og fikk høyst sannsynlig avgjørende betydning for hans senere store triumf i 1911 da han nådde Sydpolen som første mann i verden.

Den 26. august 1905 var

Amundsen in den Besitz zahlreicher Gegenstände der Eskimos, die besonders vom bekannten Polarkoch Lindstrøm verwahrt wurden. Es ist vor allem ihm zu verdanken, dass es heute im Ethnographischen Museum von Oslo eine umfangreiche Sammlung von Eskimo-Gegenständen gibt.

Die in den Wintern 1903-1905 gesammelten Erfahrungen waren für Amundsen von großem Nutzen und hatten höchst-

ed. Due to ice problems, the Gjøa and her crew had to spend yet another winter in the Arctic. Amundsen took the opportunity to make a sledge ride to Eagle City in order to announce to the world they had now sailed through the Northwest Passage. He was away from the Gjøa for 6 months, including a sledge ride lasting for

Visit onboard by the Netsilik Inuit
Besøk ombord av Netsilik-inuitene
Besuch der Netsilik-Inuitten an Bord

some 3 months. Finally, on 31st August 1906, the Gjøa reached Nome in Alaska.

By the time the Gjøa left Gjøa Haven in the summer of 1905, Amundsen had made lasting friends with the Inuit of the region, and he described the Netsilik Inuit as magnificent people of nature, and expressed the hope that civilization would never have an adverse influence on them.

Nordvestpassasjen endelig seilt gjennom for første gang og den magnetiske nordpol var blitt lokalisert og kartlagt. På grunn av isproblemer ble det imidlertid nok en overvintring for Gjøa og dens besetning. Amundsen benyttet tiden til å foreta en sledetur til Eagle City. Formålet var å meddele verden at Nordvestpassasjen var seilt gjennom. Han var borte fra Gjøa i seks måneder, inkludert en sledeferd på ca. tre måneder. Endelig kom Gjøa til Nome i Alaska 31. august 1906.

Innen Gjøa hadde forlatt Gjøahavn sommeren 1905 var det blitt varig vennskap med inuitene der, og Amundsen beskrev Netsilik-inuitene som prektige naturmennesker, og han uttrykte håp om at sivilisasjonen aldri måtte få uheldig innflytelse på dem.

wahrscheinlich entscheidende Bedeutung für seinen späteren Triumph, als er 1911 als erster Mensch den Südpol erreichte.

Am 26. August 1905 hatte man die Nordwest-Passage endlich durchquert, und der magnetische Nordpol war lokalisiert und kartiert. Probleme mit dem Eis zwangen die Gjøa und ihre Besatzung jedoch zu einer weiteren Überwinterung. Dies nutzte Amundsen zu einer Schlittenfahrt nach Eagle City, um der Welt mitzuteilen, dass die Nordwest-Passage durchquert war. Sechs Monate blieb er von der Gjøa weg, allein drei Monate hatte er für die Schlittenfahrt gebraucht. Am 31. August 1906 kam die Gjøa endlich nach Nome in Alaska.

Bevor das Schiff im Sommer 1905 Gjøahavn verlassen hatte, hatten sich tiefe freundschaftliche Beziehungen zu den dortigen Inuitten entwickelt. Amundsen beschrieb die Netsilik-Inuitten als wunderbare Naturmenschen und gab seiner Hoffnung Ausdruck, dass die Zivilisation niemals einen unglücklichen Einfluss auf sie ausüben möge.

MAUD 1918-1921 / 1922-1925

Deltagere:
1918-1921:
RoaldAmundsen
Helmer Hanssen
Oscar Wisting
Knut Sundbeck
Martin Rønne
Paul Knudsen
Peter Tessem
Emmanuel Tønnesen
Harald U. Sverdrup
Gennadij Olonkin

1922-1925:
Finn Malmgren
Oscar Wisting
Odd Dahl
Harald U. Sverdrup
Gennadij Olonkin
Kakot
Karl Hansen
S. Syvertsen

The Maud Expedition 1918-1925

Roald Amundsen's postponed North Pole expedition finally set out in July 1918. His plan was to penetrate into the pack ice north of the Bering Strait, drift with the ice as close to the North Pole as possible, so as to reach the North Pole from there, and at the same time carry out extensive scientific observations and surveys. Amundsen built a vessel similar to the Fram, naming her Maud after the Queen of Norway of the time.

Because of the World War and the Germans' ravages at sea, the Maud was forced to sail the Northeast Passage, where she encountered adverse ice conditions. It was not until July 1920 that the Maud reached the Bering

Maud-ekspedisjonen 1918-1925

Roald Amundsens utsatte Nordpols-ekspedisjon kom først avgårde i juli 1918. Planen var å gå inn i pakkisen nord for Beringstredet, drive med isen så nær Nordpolen som mulig slik at Nordpolen kunne nås, og her foreta omfattende vitenskapelige undersøkelser. Amundsen bygde et fartøy lik Fram og ga det navnet Maud etter den

Die Maud-Expedition 1918-1925

Roald Amundsens verzögerte Nordpol Expedition konnte erst im Juli 1918 beginnen. Der ursprüngliche Plan sah vor, nördlich der Beringstraße ins Packeis vorzudringen und dann mit dem Eis so nah wie möglich an den Nordpol zu treiben. So wollte man den Nordpol erreichen und dort umfangreiche wissensch aftliche Untersuchungen vornehmen. Amundsen ließ ein Schiff ähnlich der Fram bauen und gab ihm nach der damaligen norwegischen Königin den Namen Maud.

Wegen des Weltkriegs und der besonders gefährlichen Situation auf den Meeren musste die Maud den Weg durch die Nordost-Passage einschlagen. Hier traf sie auf

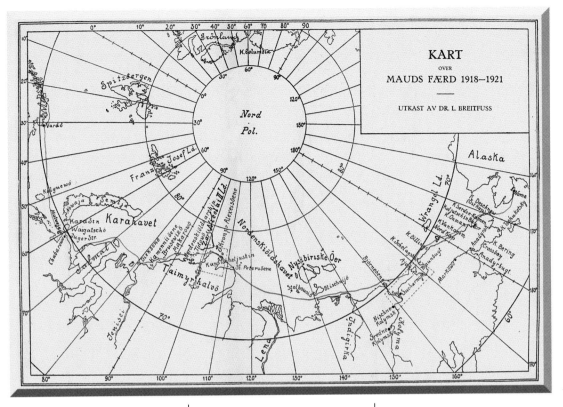

Map of the Maud expedition 1918-1921

Kart over Mauds ferd 1918-1921

Karte über die Fahrt der Maud 1918-1921

Strait.

Following a short stay on the Alaskan coast, the Maud made an attempt to penetrate northwards into the pack ice, but was driven southwards towards the Siberian coast and compelled to winter once again. During that winter, two of the men carried out a 2,000 km sledge expedition around the Chukchi Peninsula.

The Maud suffered damage from the enormous pressures of the pack ice, and had to sail for Seattle in 1921 for repairs. In June 1922, the Maud headed north once again, putting Roald Amundsen

davoerende norske dronningen.

På grunn av verdenskrigen, og tyskernes herjinger på havet, måtte Maud ta veien gjennom Nordøstpassasjen. Der møtte det vanskelige isforhold. Først i juli 1920 nådde Maud Beringstredet.

Etter et kort opphold på Alaskakysten gjorde Maud et forsøk på å trenge nordover inn i pakkisen, men fartøyet ble ført mot Sibirkysten og fikk en ny overvintring. Herunder foretok to menn et nesten 2000 km. langt slede-tokt rundt Tsjuktsji-halvøya.

Maud var blitt skadet under ispresset og måtte i

schwierige Eis Verhältnisse. Erst im Juli 1920 gelangte die Maud in die Beringstraße.

Nach einem kurzen Aufenthalt an der Küste Alaskas machte die Maud den Versuch, nach Norden ins Packeis vorzudringen. Das Schiff wurde jedoch an die sibirische Küste getrieben und musste dort ein weiteres Mal überwintern. Während dieser Zeit bewältigten zwei Männer der Expedition eine fast 2000 km lange Schlittenfahrt um die Tschuktschenhalbinsel.

Unter dem Druck des Eises war die Maud beschädigt worden und musste deshalb

ashore on the Alaskan coast with an aeroplane that was later to crash.

Amundsen had also placed another aeroplane onboard the Maud. With Odd Dahl at the stick, this plane was to make four flights, two ending in minor crashes and the fourth in the total wreck of

1921 seile til Seattle for reparasjon. I juni 1922 gikk Maud nordover igjen og satte først i land Roald Amundsen på Alaskakysten med et fly som senere havarerte.

Amundsen hadde også plassert et fly om bord i Maud og med Odd Dahl bak spaken ble det foretatt fire

1921 Seattle anlaufen, um repariert zu werden. Im Juni 1922 brach die Maud wieder nach Norden auf und setzte Roald Amundsen an der Küste Alaskas an Land - mit einem Flugzeug, das später havarierte.

Amundsen hatte auch an Bord der Maud ein Flugzeug

Equipment for 40 days was always packed and ready to go

Utstyr for 40 døgn sto alltid ferdigpakket

Ausrüstung für 40 Tage stand immer bereit.

the plane. These flights were the first ever carried out in Polar Regions, and the first to be undertaken with a ship as base. The lessons learned from these experiences led to a clearer recognition of the difficulties of landing and taking off, and it was seen

flyvninger. To av disse resulterte i mindre havarier og ved den fjerde havarerte flyet totalt. Dette var av de første flyvninger i polare områder og de første med utgangspunkt fra et fartøy. Av flygningene lærte man å se på avgangs- og landings-

mitgebracht. Mit Odd Dahl am Steuerknüppel wurden drei Flüge unternommen. Zwei davon endeten mit kleineren Abstürzen, der dritte mit Totalschaden. Diese drei Versuche gehörten zu den ersten Flügen in Polar-Gebieten – die ersten über-

that navigating in Polar Regions was extremely difficult.

The Maud, under Oscar Wisting's command, continued northwards into the pack ice, but the ice drift instead drove the ship towards the New Siberian Islands, and the Maud never came anywhere

Roald Amundsen in the lounge on Maud
Roald Amundsen i salongen på Maud
Roald Amundsen im Salon der Maud

near its ultimate goal, the North Pole. Amundsen instructed the Maud to turn back, and she had, once again, to pound her way back to the Bering Strait, which she reached in August 1925, after a further three years in the ice.

Although Roald Amundsen failed to reach the North Pole with the Maud, extensive and valuable surveys were carried out under Harald U. Sverdrup's command, thereby making the Maud expedition one of the most significant of its time.

muligheten med nye øyne og fant at navigasjon i polare områder bød på store vanskeligheter.

Maud fortsatte nordover inn i pakkisen under ledelse av Oscar Wisting, men isdriften førte fartøyet til Ny-Sibirøyene istedenfor og kom ikke i nærheten av sitt mål, Nordpolen. Maud fikk beskjed fra Amundsen om å snu, og måtte igjen stampe seg tilbake mot Beringstredet som ble nådd i august 1925, etter tre nye år i isen.

Selv om Roald Amundsen mislyktes i å komme til Nordpolen med Maud, ble det utført meget omfattende og resultatrike undersøkelser under Harald U. Sverdrups ledelse, og det har gitt Maud-ekspedisjonen status som en av de viktigste i sin tid.

haupt, die ihren Ausgangspunkt auf einem Schiff hatten. Als wichtiges Resultat dieser Versuche lernte man die völlig anderen Start- und Landemöglichkeiten kennen und stellte fest, dass Landungen auf dem Polareis große Schwierigkeiten mit sich führten.

Unter dem Kommando von Oscar Wisting setzte die Maud ihre Reise nach Norden ins Packeis fort. Das Treibeis führte das Schiff jedoch zu den Neusibirischen Inseln, und es kam nicht einmal in die Nähe seines Zieles, des Nordpols. Amundsen übermittelte dem Schiff das Kommando umzukehren, und wieder musste es sich den Weg zurück zur Beringstraße bahnen. Nach drei weiteren Jahren im Eis erreichte das Schiff im August 1925 die Beringstraße.

Obwohl es Roald Amundsen nicht gelungen war, mit der Maud zum Nordpol vorzudringen, wurden unter der Leitung von Harald U. Sverdrup ebenso umfassende wie aufschlussreiche Untersuchungen durchgeführt, so dass die Maud-Expedition zu einer der wichtigsten Forschungsreisen ihrer Zeit wurde.

Deltagere	Umberto Nobile
N24:	Hjalmar Riiser-Larsen
Leif Dietrichson	Fredrik Ramm
Oscar Omdal	Birger Gottwaldt
Lincoln Ellsworth	Emil Horgen
	Oscar Wisting
N25:	Oskar Omdal
Hjalmar Riiser-Larsen	Finn Malmgren
Roald Amundsen	Fridtjof Storm-Johnsen
Karl Feucht	Natale Cecioni
	Ettore Arduino
NORGE:	Vicenzo Pomella
Roald Amundsen	Renato Alessandrini
Lincoln Ellsworth	Attilio Caratti

Roald Amundsen the aviator

Roald Amundsen became interested in aeroplanes at an early age. Already in 1913, when the Fram was lying in Colon waiting to pass through the Panama Canal, he wrote the following to Doxrud, then master of the Fram: «The expedition is to have two hydro-planes and the Swedish aviator Cederstrøm will be coming along.»

The 11th June 1914 was a big day in Amundsen's life. It was the day he passed his flying test, obtaining his civilian pilot's licence with the number 1 in September 1915. The Maud's first voyage through the Northeast Passage had met with limited success, and Amundsen went ashore in 1921. His finances were shaky.

Roald Amundsen tar fly i bruk

Roald Amundsen fattet meget tidlig interesse for fly. Allerede da Fram lå i Colon i 1913 og ventet på å komme gjennom Panamakanalen skrev han følgende til Doxrud som på den tiden var skipper på Fram: «Ekspedisjonen får to hydro aeroplaner, og den svenske aviator Cederstrøm følger med.»

Den 11. juni 1914 var en stor dag i Amundsens liv. På denne dagen besto han flyprøven og fikk sivilt flysertifikat nummer l i september 1915. Mauds første ferd gjennom Nordøstpassasjen hadde vært en betinget suksess, og Amundsen gikk i land i 1921. Hans økonomi var i uorden. Verdenskrigen hadde

Roald Amundsen als Pilot

Das Interesse am Fliegen wurde bei Roald Amundsen bereits früh geweckt. Schon als die Fram 1913 in Colon lag und auf die Passage durch den Panamakanal wartete, schrieb er folgende Zeilen an Doxrud, der zu dieser Zeit Kapitän der Fram war: «Die Expedition bekommt zwei Wasserflugzeuge, und der schwedische Flugtechniker Cederström begleitet sie.»

Der 11. Juni 1914 war ein großer Tag im Leben Roald Amundsens. An diesem Tag bestand er die Flugprüfung, und im September 1915 bekam er den zivilen Pilotenschein Nr. l. Die erste Reise der Maud durch die Nordost-Passage war nur teilweise ein Erfolg, und

However, World War One had brought about substantial technical advances in the field of aviation. Amundsen was convinced that the aeroplane was the perfect tool of

imidlertid skapt stor fremgang på det flytekniske området. Amundsen var overbevist om at flyet var den nye tids redskap for å drive oppdagelser i polar områdene.

Amundsen ging 1921 an Land. Seine finanzielle Lage war schlecht. Der Weltkrieg hatte jedoch auf dem Gebiet der Flugtechnik für große Fortschritte gesorgt.

1. Accident during test flight
2. N25 ready for takeoff
3. Safely back after three weeks on the ice
4. N25 en route to Oslo

1. Havari under flyprøven
2. N25 klargjøres
3. Vel tilbake etter tre uker i isen
4. N25 på vei til Oslo

1. Bruchlandung beim Probeflug
2. N25 wird aufgeputzt
3. Heil zurück nach drei Wochen im Eis
4. N25 auf dem Weg nach Oslo

modern times for exploring the Arctic regions.

In 1922, Roald Amundsen purchased a Junkers plane; it was soon wrecked, so he bought a new one. His plan was to fly this new plane from Wainwright to Svalbard. The plan to fly to Svalbard failed and the aeroplane was a complete write-off. The financial position worsened. He statio-

I 1922 kjøpte Roald Amundsen en junkersmaskin som imidlertid havarerte. Han kjøpte en ny og med den nye maskinen var det hans plan å fly fra Wainwright til Svalbard. Planen om å fly til Svalbard mislyktes og flyet totalhavarerte. Den økonomiske stillingen forverret seg. Om bord i Maud plasserte han et mindre fly av typen

Amundsen war überzeugt, dass Flugzeuge für die Entdeckung der Polargebiete in Zukunft wichtig sein werden.

Im Jahr 1922 kaufte Amundsen eine Maschine vom Typ Junker, die allerdings Totalschaden erlitt. Er kaufte daher eine neue und mit der neuen Maschine wollte er seinen Plan ver-

ned a smaller Curtis Oriol aeroplane onboard.

In 1924, his financial position had become totally intolerable. There was not enough capital to commission an air expedition aimed at carrying out the first transpolar flight over the North Pole, in order

Curtis Oriol.

I 1924 var den økonomiske situasjonen blitt helt uholdbar. Det eksisterte ikke kapital til å utruste en fly ekspedisjon for å foreta den første transpolare flight over Nordpolen for å fastslå om det fantes fastland i området.

wirklichen, von Wainwright nach Spitzbergen zu fliegen. Der Plan, nach Svalbard zu fliegen, missglückte, da auch dieses Flugzeug Totalschaden erlitt. Die finanzielle Seite verschlechterte sich. Er brachte ein kleineres Flugzeug vom Typ Curtis

The airship Norge (Norway)

Luftskipet Norge

Das Luftschiff Norge (Norwegen)

to establish once and for all whether there was in fact land in the area. Amundsen came into contact with the American capitalist, Lincoln Ellsworth, who provided the necessary capital to purchase two Dornier Wal planes, registered as N24 and N25. With the support of «The Aviation Society», among

Men når nøden er størst er hjelpen gjerne nærmest. Amundsen kom i kontakt med den amerikanske rikmannen Lincoln Ellsworth. Han skaffet midler til kjøp av to Dornier Walmaskiner, registrert som N.24 og N.25. Med støtte fra bl.a. Luftseilasforeningen ble disse utrustet, og avgang fra Kings

Oriol an Bord der Maud.

1924 war seine wirtschaftliche Lage nicht mehr tragbar. Es gab kein Kapital mehr für die Ausrüstung einer Flugexpedition. Eine solche Expedition sollte den ersten transpolaren Flug über den Nordpol durchführen um festzustellen, ob es in diesem Gebiet Festland gab. Wenn

others, these two aircraft were equipped for polar flights and took off from King's Bay in Svalbard on 21st May 1925. After 8 hours in the air, both planes were forced to make emergency landings due to engine trouble on the N25. This was to be the beginning of a gruelling 4-week stopover on the ice at 88 degrees north - a new «Furthest North» record.

Following severe hardship and toil to level an airstrip,

En route to Seattle
På vei mot Seattle
Auf dem Weg nach Seattle

Riiser-Larsen succeeded in taking off with the N25, with six men on board. They managed to reach a fjord on the coast of Nordaustlandet before running out of fuel. This is one of the most exciting episodes in the history of aviation.

Bay på Svalbard fant sted 21. mai 1925. Etter åtte timers flyging måtte begge nødlande fordi N. 25 fikk motortrøbbel. Dette ble innledningen til et fire ukers langt dramatisk opphold i isen på 88 grader nordlig bredde.

Etter å ha gått gjennom en del dramatiske episoder samt å hatt store strabaser forbundet med å lage en flystripe, klarte Riiser-Larsen å ta av med seks menn med N.25.

Roald Amundsen hadde ikke oppnådd sin hensikt; han var ikke kommet til Nordpolen og hadde heller ikke foretatt en transpolar flight. Men etter anbefaling fra Riiser-Larsen, anskaffet han luftskipet Norge som var konstruert og ført av den daværende italienske oberst Nobile. Med luftskipet Norge ble det foretatt en vellykket transpolar flight som tok 72

aber die Not am größten ist, ist Hilfe nicht weit. Amundsen lernte den reichen Amerikaner Lincoln Ellsworth kennen, der ihm das Kapital zum Kauf zweier Dornier Wal-Maschinen - zugelassen mit den laufenden Nummern 24 und 25 - be-schaffte. Diese wurden u.a. mit Unterstützung des norwegischen Luftfahrtvereins ausgerüstet, und am 21. Mai 1925 erfolgte der Start in Kings Bay auf Spitzbergen. Nach acht Stunden Flug mussten beide Maschinen notlanden, weil in der Nr. 25 ein Motorschaden enstanden war. Dies war der Anfang eines vierwöchigen dramatischen Aufenthaltes im Eis - auf 88 Grad nördlicher Breite, was übrigens ein neuer «dem Nordpol am nächsten»- Rekord war. Nach großen Strapazen bei der Einebnung einer Startbahn gelang es Riiser-Larsen, die Nummer 25 mit sechs Mann Besatzung in die Luft zu bringen. Er erreichte einen Fjord im Nordostland, bevor der Treibstofftank leer war. Dies war sicherlich eine der spannendsten Episoden in der Geschichte der Luftfahrt.

Roald Amundsen hatte sein Ziel nicht erreicht. Er war weder zum Nordpol gekommen, noch hatte er einen Transpolarflug geschafft. Riiber-Larsen empfahl ihm

Roald Amundsen had not fulfilled his plans - he had not reached the North Pole, nor had he succeeded in carrying out a transpolar flight. However, following Riiser-Larsen's advice, he purchased the airship Norge, designed, constructed and commanded by Colonel Nobile. The Norge did succeed in making one transpolar flight lasting 72 hours. Its point of departure was King's Bay on Svalbard, where it left on 11th May 1926. After 72 hours in the air and several dramatic incidents, the airship Norge landed in Teller, Alaska on 14th May.

It had been established that there was neither land nor new islands to be seen in the areas flown over by the Norge. The airship's voyage also formed the basis for something to come later. Riiser-Larsen wrote in his account: «And when the time comes when no one can write to me any longer, no one will set out on voyages of discovery in Polar Regions any more. Then, air routes will follow the great circles, unaffected by the Arctic.»

timer. Avgangsstedet var Kings Bay på Svalbard, og herfra fant avgangen sted 11. mai 1926. Etter 72 timer i luften, og mange dramatiske episoder underveis, landet luftskipet Norge i Teller i Alaska 14. mai.

Det ble fastslått at det fantes hverken fastland eller øyer i de områdene som Norge

fløy over. Luftskipets ferd dannet også grunnlaget for noe som skulle komme senere. Riiser-Larsen skrev bl.a. i sin beretning: «Og når den tid kommer at man ikke kan skrive til meg mer, da reiser man ikke lenger på oppdagelsesreiser i arktiske egne. Da går luftrutene etter storsirklene, uanfektet Arktis.»

jedoch, das von dem damaligen Oberst Nobile konstruierte und geführte Luftschiff Norge zu kaufen. Mit dem Luftschiff Norge gelang ein Flug über den Pol, der 72 Stunden dauerte. Der Start erfolgte am 11. Mai 1926 in Kings Bay auf Spitzbergen, und nach 72 Stunden in der Luft und vielen dramatischen Episoden landete das Luftschiff Norge am 14. Mai in Teller, Alaska.

Es wurde festgestellt, dass es weder Festland noch neue Inseln in dem Gebiet gab, das Norge überflogen hatte. Diese Reise des Luftschiffes war auch die Grundlage für etwas, was erst viel später kommen sollte. Riiser-Larsen schreibt in seinem Bericht u.a. folgendes: «Und wenn die Zeit so weit fortgeschritten ist, dass man mir keine Briefe mehr schreiben kann, wird man keine Entdeckungsreisen in arktischen Gegenden mehr machen. Dann werden die Fluglinien unabhängig von der Arktis den großen Zirkeln folgen.»

Deltagere:

Rene Guilbaud
Roald Amundsen
Leif Dietrichson
Albert de Cuverville
Gilbert Brazy
Emile Valett

Latham
the Italian tragedy

Following the Norge voyage, Amundsen stated:

«I shall now stop my work and leave it to others to carry on, but should anyone in the North or South need my help, I am at their disposal.»

With the airship Italia; Nobile flew from Kings Bay to the North Pole on 23rd May 1928. On the return journey, the airship crashed north-northeast of Nordaustlandet. The gondola was knocked off following a collision with what later came to be known as the White Bear Floe. Nobile and 9 men found themselves marooned on the ice floe, and the airship flew on with 6 men on board; they were never found.

The Italia tragedy resulted

Latham
Italiatragedien

Etter Norgesferden uttalte Amundsen:

«Nu legger jeg opp, nu får andre fortsette, men skulle nogen i Nord eller Syd trenge min hjelp, står jeg til tjeneste.»

Med luftskipet Italia fløy Nobile fra Kings Bay til Nordpolen den 23. mai 1928. På returen havarerte han NNØ for Nordaustlandet. Gondolen ble slått av ved kollisjonen med det som senere ble kjent som Den Hvite Bjørns Flak. Nobile og ni menn befant seg på flaket. Luftskipet fortsatte med seks menn om bord, disse ble aldri funnet.

Italiatragedien førte til en redningsaksjon av store dimensjoner. I alt deltok sju nasjoner med 22 fly og 15

Latham
die Italia-Tragödie

Nach dem Flug mit dem Luftschiff Norge sagte Amundsen:

«Jetzt höre ich auf, mögen andere weitermachen. Sollte aber jemand im Norden oder Süden meine Hilfe brauchen, stehe ich zu Diensten.»

Mit dem Luftschiff Italia brach Nobile am 23. Mai 1928 von Kings Bay in Richtung Nordpol auf. Auf der Rückfahrt havarierte das Schiff nordnordöstlich des Nordostlandes. Die Gondel wurde beim Aufprall auf die Stelle, die später als «die Eisscholle des weißen Bären» bekannt wurde, abgeschlagen. Nobile und neun Besatzungsmitglieder befanden sich auf der Scholle. Sechs Mann blieben an Bord

in an enormous rescue operation. It involved seven nations, 22 aeroplanes, 15 vessels and a total of 1,400 men. Nobile's camp was found on 19th June. He was rescued from the ice floe by the Swedish aviator Lundborg on 24th June. The remaining survivors were picked up by the Russian icebreaker Krassin on 11th June.

It was natural to call on

fartøyer med til sammen 1400 menn. Nobiles leir ble funnet den 19. juni. Han ble reddet fra isflaket av den svenske flyveren Lundborg den 24. juni. Resten av de overlevende ble tatt opp av den russiske isbryteren Krassin 11. juni.

Som et ledd i redningsaksjonen var det naturlig å kalle på Amundsen. Hans svar på om han kunne

des Luftschiffes und wurden niemals gefunden.

Die Italien-Katastrofe führte zu einer Rettungsaktion von großem Format. Insgesamt beteiligten sich 7 Länder mit 22 Flugzeugen, 15 Fahrzeugen und insgesamt 1400 Mann. Nobiles Lager wurde am 19. Juni entdeckt. Es war auf einem Eisschollen und wurde vom schwedis-

Viglieri by «The Red Tent» on «The White Bear's Floe»

Viglieri ved «Det røde telt» på «Den hvite bjørns flak»

Viglieri am «Roten Zelt» auf der «Eisscholle des weißen Bären»

Amundsen for help as part of the rescue efforts. His answer to the question of when he could come was: «Right away!» He requested that a Dornier Wal flying boat, of the same type as the N25, be placed at his disposal. This was not possible. The French, however, declared their willingness to provide the Latham, a flying boat, which

komme var «Right away». Han ønsket at det skulle stilles til disposisjon en Dornier Wal flybåt, av samme type som N. 25. Dette lyktes ikke. Derimot sa franskmennene seg villige til å stille Latham til rådighet, en flybåt som ikke var spesielt egnet til formålet. Guilbaud, føreren av Latham, kom til Bergen 16.juni. Dietrichson,

chen Flieger Lundborg am 24. Juni gerettet. Die anderen Überlebenden wurden vom russischen Eisbrecher Krassin am 11. Juni aufgenommen.

In dieser Situation war es naheliegend, Amundsen um Hilfe zu bitten. Seine positive Antwort war der kurze Bescheid: «Right away». Man sollte ihm ein Dornier Wal-Flugboot desselben Typs wie

was not particularly suited for the task at hand. Guilbaud, commander of the Latham arrived in Bergen on 16th June. Dietrichson, Amundsen and Wisting reached Bergen at the same time. They travelled on to Tromsø on 18th June, which they subsequently left at 4 p.m. Radio contact was broken after 2 3/4 hours. The «Latham» probably cras-

Amundsen og Wisting kom til Bergen samtidig. Ferden gikk til Tromsø den 18.juni med flyavgang herfra klokken 16.00. Radioforbindelsen ble brutt etter 2 timer og 45 minutter. Latham havarerte trolig mellom kl. 18.45 og 19.15 i nærheten av Bjørnøya. Nå måtte Amundsen også ettersøkes.

Store områder ble

Nr. 25 zur Verfügung stellen, was aber nicht gelang. Die Franzosen hingegen waren bereit, eine Latham-Maschine zu schicken, obwohl dieses Flugboot für diesen Zweck nicht besonders geeignet war. Der Pilot der Latham, kam am 16. Juni in Bergen an. Dietrichson, Amundsen und Wisting kamen zur gleichen Zeit nach Bergen. Die Reise

1. Nobile and Titina after the rescue
2. Lundborg at the radio camp
3. Roald Amundsen prior to departing Tromsø.

1. Nobile og Titina etter redningen
2. Lundborg i radioleiren
3. Roald Amundsen før starten fra Tromsø.

1. Nobile und Titina nach der Rettung
2. Lundborg im Radiolager
3. Roald Amundsen vor der Abreise aus Tromsø.

hed between 6.45 and 7.15 p.m., in the vicinity of Bjørnøya. Now a search had to be started for Amundsen as well.

Vast areas were searched and considerable resources devoted, but to no avail.

The Norwegians refused to believe that Amundsen had been killed. He had been

gjennomsøkt og betydelige ressurser anvendt forgjeves.

At Amundsen var omkommet nektet nordmennene å tro. Han hadde vært borte i 26 dager med N.25. Man håpet i det lengste, men håpet forsvant gradvis. Den 28. august drev det i land en vingeflottør fra Latham. (Et hull i en vingeflottør

führte sie am 18. Juni zunächst nach Tromsø, von wo aus sie um 16 Uhr starteten. Die Radioverbindung wurde nach 2 Stunden und 45 Minuten unterbrochen. Die «Latham» havarierte wahr-scheinlich zwischen 18.45 und 19.15 Uhr auf halber Strecke zwischen Tromsø und der Bäreninsel. Jetzt mus-

away for 26 days with the N25. Everyone kept hoping till the very last, but hope gradually vanished. On 28th August a wing float from the «Latham» drifted ashore (a hole in a wing float had been repaired in Tromsø).
Now all hope was gone. Some time later a fuel tank was found west of Namsos. It was the only tank that, with considerable effort, could be removed. A damaged wing float with a similar tank had previously been replaced on an aeroplane of the same type. They were strong indications that a similar attempt had been made with the Latham, but this time without success.

On 14th December, 17 years after he had planted the Norwegian flag on the South Pole together with 4 other men, an official day of remembrance was held to commemorate Amundsen. Roald Amundsen was only 55 years old.

hadde vært reparert i Tromsø.) Nå var alt håp ute. Senere ble det funnet en bensintank vest for Namsos. Det var den eneste tanken, som med en del arbeid kunne tas ut. Tidligere hadde man på et fly av samme sort skiftet ut en skadet vingeflottør med tilsvarende tank. Mange ting tydet på at man hadde forsøkt det samme på Latham, men ikke lykkes.

Den 14.desember - 17 år etter at han sammen med sine fire menn plantet det norske flagget på Sydpolen ble det arrangert en offisiell minnedag for Amundsen. Roald Amundsen ble bare 55 år gammel.

ste auch Amundsen gesucht werden. Große Gebiete wurden abgesucht, alle verfügbaren Mittel und Kräfte eingesetzt – vergeblich.

Dass Amundsen umgekommen war, wollten die Norweger nicht glauben. Seit 26 Tagen war er mit Nr. 25 verschwunden. Bis zuletzt hoffte man, doch mit jedem Tag schwand auch die Hoffnung. Am 28. August wurde ein Schwimmer der Latham an Land getrieben (Ein Loch in einem Schwimmer war noch in Tromsø repariert worden). Damit war auch der letzte Funken Hoffnung verschwunden. Später wurde westlich von Namsos ein Benzintank gefunden. Dies war der einzige Tank, der mit einiger Arbeit ausgebaut werden konnte. Schon früher hatte man bei einem Flugzeug ähnlichen Modells einen be-schädigten Schwimmer durch einen entsprechenden Tank ersetzt. Vieles spricht dafür, dass etwas ähnliches mit der Latham versucht wurde, aber nicht gelang.

Am 14. Dezember – 17 Jahre, nachdem er zusammen mit seinen vier Begleitern die norwegische Flagge am Südpol ins Eis gebohrt hatte, - wurde ein offizieller Gedenktag für Amundsen arrangiert. Roald Amundsen wurde nur 55 Jahre alt.

The Fram Museum

Norway is an Arctic nation. More than 40% of its territory lies north of the Arctic Circle. Svalbard, Jan Mayen, Bjørnøya and many small islands are Norwegian territory. Norway claims approximately 2 million square kilometres of the Antarctic continent in the south. Bouveøya is Norwegian territory. It is therefore natural that Norway has participated in many important expeditions to both the Arctic and the Antarctic. The Fram Museum contains exhibitions of the most famous expeditions that were of global historical significance. The centrepiece of the museum is of course the world's strongest wooden ship, the Polar ship Fram, which the public can board

Frammuseet

Norge er en polarnasjon med mer enn 40% av land-områdene nord for Polar-sirkelen. Svalbard, Jan Mayen, Bjørnøya, og flere småøyer er norsk territorium. I syd gjør Norge krav på ca. 2 millioner kvadratkilometer av det antarktiske kontinentet. Bouveøya er norsk terri-torium. Det er derfor naturlig at Norge har deltatt i mange og betydningsfulle eks-pedisjoner til både Arktis og Antarktis. Presentasjoner av de mest kjente ekspedisjone-ne, som alle er av verdens-historisk betydning er samlet i Frammuseet. Det selvfølgelige midtpunktet i museet er verdens sterkeste treskute Polarskipet Fram, som publi-kum kan gå ombord i og se på lugarene, salongene, mes-

Das Fram Museum

Norwegen ist eine Polarnation mit über 40 % seiner Landgebiete nördlich des Polarzirkels. Svalbard, Jan Mayen, die Bäreninsel und mehrere kleinere Inseln gehören zu norwegischem Hoheitsgebiet. Im Süden beansprucht Norwegen ca. 2 Millionen Quadratkilometer des antarktischen Kontinents. Deshalb ist es einleuchtend, dass Norwegen an vielen und bedeutenden Expeditionen zum Nord- und Südpol teilgenommen hat. Errungenschaften der bedeutendsten Expeditionen, die alle von welt-geschichtlicher Bedeutung sind, wurden im Fram-Museum gesammelt. Mittelpunkt des Museums bildet natürlich das stärkste

and take a look around its cabins, lounges, mess room, cargo hold and engine room.

The Fram returned home from Buenos Aires in 1914 and was moored at Horten, exposed to the wind and weather. After World War One was over a number of committees worked on preserving Fram, but without results. The project's strongest proponent, Otto Sverdrup, was elected as the chairman of the Fram Committee in 1925. He struggled on untiringly together with the committee's members and several other key people. In 1929 Fram was towed to Framnæs Mekaniske Verksted in Sandefjord. Here, under Otto Sverdrup's supervision, the ship was repaired with the excellent support of Consul Lars Christensen.

In 1930 Fram was finally restored to the condition it was in during Otto Sverdrup's expedition to the islands to the northwest of Greenland. Otto Sverdrup died in the same year Fram participated in a large exhibition in Trondheim. It took a long time before Fram finally got a permanent home. In 1934 the Oslo Association of Architects offered to hold an architecture competition to design a building for the honoured vessel.60 entries were submitted and the winner was an architect

sen, lasterommet og maskinrommet.

Fram kom hjem fra Buenos Aires i 1914 og ble liggende i Horten utsatt for vær og vind. Etter at 1. verdenskrig var over, arbeidet en rekke komiteer med å bevare Fram, men uten resultat. Sakens sterkeste talsmann, Otto Sverdrup ble valgt til formann i Framkomiteen i 1925. Han arbeidet utrettelig videre sammen med komiteens medlemmer og flere andre sentrale personer. I 1929 ble Fram tauet til Framnæs Mekaniske Verksted i Sandefjord. Med god støtte fra konsul Lars Christensen, og under Otto Sverdrups tilsyn, ble skuta reparert.

I 1930 var Fram ferdig restaurert i den skikk den var under Otto Sverdrups ferd til øyene nordvest for Grønland. Samme året som Fram deltok på en stor utstilling i Tronheim døde Otto Sverdrup. Det gikk lang tid før Fram fikk sitt endelige hjem. I 1934 tilbød Oslo Arkitektforening seg å lage en konkurranse for et bygg til æresskuta. Det kom inn 60 utkast og vinneren ble arkitekt Bjarne Tøien med mottoet «Saga».

Som en kuriositet kan det nevnes at Fram ble trukket inn i sitt nye hjem av en elektrisk motor. Skuta beveget seg med en cm. per minutt. Den

Holzschiff der Welt, die Fram. Besucher können an Bord gehen und sich die Kajüten, Salons, Messen, Last- und Maschinenraum ansehen.

1914 kam Fram aus Buenos Aires zurück und war Wind und Wetter ausgesetzt, als sie in Horten vor Anker lag. Nach Ende des ersten Weltkriegs arbeiteten mehrere Ausschüsse erfolglos daran, die Fram zu bewahren. Der größte Befürworter des Projekts, Otto Sverdrup, wurde 1925 zum Vorsitzenden im Fram-Komitee gewählt. Unermüdlich arbeitete er mit den Mitgliedern des Ausschusses sowie mehreren anderen wichtigen Persönlichkeiten weiter. 1929 wurde die Fram zur Werft Framnæs Mekaniske Verksted in Sandefjord geschleppt. Unterstützt vom Konsul Lars Christensen und unter der Aufsicht von Otto Sverdrup, wurde das Schiff in Stand gesetzt.

1930 stand die Fram wieder so da, wie sie unter der Führung von Otto Sverdrup zu den Inseln nordwestlich von Grönland auslegte. Im gleichen Jahr als die Fram an einer Ausstellung in Trondheim teilnahm, starb Otto Sverdrup. Es sollte lange dauern, bevor die Fram einen entgültigen Standort erhalten sollte. 1934 bot Oslo

called Bjarne Tøien with his entry, «Saga».

Fram was pulled into its new home by an electric motor. The ship moved one

20. mai 1936 kunne Frammuseet endelig innvies. Både Hans Majestet Kong Haakon VII og Hans Konglige Høyhet Kronprins

Arkitektforening an, einen Wettbewerb auszuschreiben, um ein Gebäude für das ehrenvolle Schiff zu zeichnen. Es kamen 60 Entwürfe, und

centimetre per minute. On 20th May 1936 the Fram Museum was finally open. Both His Majesty King Haakon VII and His Royal Highness Crown Prince Olav were present. A national monument was finally in place.

The museum is located on Bygdøy, a short distance from Oslo and is easily accessible by bus or, in the summer season, ferry from the City Hall quayside. Its closest neighbours are the Kon-Tiki Museum and the Norwegian

Olav var tilstede. Et nasjonalmonument var nå kommet på plass.

Museet ligger på Bygdøy med kort avstand fra Oslo og er lett tilgjengelig med buss eller ferje i sommersesongen fra Rådhusbryggen. Kon-Tiki Museet og Norsk Sjøfartsmuseum ligger som nære naboer, og Vikingskipshuset og Norsk Folkemuseum ligger innen 15 minutters gangavstand. Halvøya Bygdøy blir derfor populært kalt Museumshalvøya og er en av hovedattraksjonene i Oslo.

der Sieger war der Architekt Bjarne Tøien unter dem Titel "Sage".

Interessant ist auch, dass die Fram in ihr neues Heim mit einem elektrischen Motor –1 cm pro Minute - gezogen wurde. Am 20. Mai 1936 konnte das Gebäude endlich eingeweiht werden. Sowohl Seine Majestät König Haakon VII. wie auch seine königliche Hoheit Kronprinz Olav waren anwesend. Ein nationales Denkmal war errichtet worden.

Das Museum befindet sich

Maritime Museum. The Viking Ship Museum and the Norwegian Folk Museum are within 15 minutes walk. The Bygdøy peninsula is therefore popularly known as the Museum Peninsula and is one of Oslo's main attractions. The area in itself is an attraction with, among other things, its rich hiking and recreational areas and the opportunities it provides for bathing in the sea. It is also home to His Majesty the King's summer residence, Kongsgården.

The number of visitors has varied from 18,000 the year it opened down to 5,000 during World War Two, 1940-1945. After the war the number of visitors increased annually and in 1994 we achieved the current record of 267,500 visitors. On 5th August 1999, the member of total visitors reached 10,000,000. During the last ten years the average number of visitors has been 250,000. A large number of tourists visit the museum. The tourists come from all over the world though most come from the Scandinavian countries, France, Germany, Italy, and, in the last few years, Spain.

The main exhibition has explanatory texts in eight languages and describes the expeditions of our three great polar heroes, Nansen, Sverdrup and Amundsen.

Området i seg selv er en attraksjon med blant annet rike tur- og fri-arealer og bademuligheter i sjøen. H.M. Kongens sommerresidens, Kongsgården ligger også her.

Besøket har variert fra 18 000 i åpningsåret og ned til 5000 under krigen i 1940-1945. Etter krigen økte besøkstallet årlig og nådde i 1994 en foreløpig rekord på 267 500 besøkende. Den 5. august 1999 passerte besøkende nr. 10 000 000. De siste ti årene har besøket ligget på gjennomsnittlig 250 000 per år. Et stort antall turister oppsøker museet. Turistene kommer fra hele verden med hovedvekt på de skandinaviske landene, Frankrike, Tyskland, Italia og i de senere år også Spania.

Hovedutstillingen som er tekstet på åtte språk beskriver ferdene til våre tre store polarhelter, Nansen, Sverdrup og Amundsen. Rundt skuta er det utstillinger av gjenstander som har vært med på ferdene.

auf der Halbinsel Bygdøy unweit von Oslo, und man erreicht sie im Sommer leicht mit Bus oder Fähre vom Kai Rådhusbryggen. Das Kon-Tiki Museum und das norwegische Seefahrtsmuseum sind die nächsten Nachbarn und nur 15 Minuten Fußweg braucht man zum Wikingerschiffhaus und dem Freilichtmuseum Norsk Folkemuseum. Im Volksmund nennt man die Halbinsel auch oft die Museumshalbinsel – eine der Hauptattraktionen in Oslo. Die Halbinsel bietet außerdem schöne Wander- und Badegebiete. Auch die Sommerresidenz des Königs, Kongsgården, befindet sich hier.

Die Besucherzahlen gingen von 18.000 im Eröffnungsjahr auf nur 5000 während des zweiten Weltkriegs zurück. Nach dem Krieg stiegen die Zahlen jährlich, bis sie 1994 den vorläufigen Rekord von 276.000 erreichten. Am 5. August 1999 kam der 10.000.000. Besucher. In den letzten zehn Jahren lagen die Besucherzahlen durchschnittlich bei 250.000 jährlich. Viele der Besucher sind Touristen aus der ganzen Welt. Die meisten Besucher kommen aus Skandinavien, Frankreich, Deutschland und in den letzten Jahren auch aus Spanien.

Photo of the quarterdeck and exhibits
Bilde av akterdekket og gjenstander fra utstillingen
Bild des Achterdecks und der Gegenstände aus der Ausstellung

Photo of the fore deck and exhibits
Bilde av fordekket og gjenstander fra utstillingen
Bild des Vorderdecks und der Gegenstände aus der Ausstellung

Photo of the galley and exhibits
Bilde av byssa og gjenstander fra utstillingen
Bild der Kombüse und der Gegenstände aus der Ausstellung